THE MAP TO

MW00824428

HOW TO NAVIGATE THE ART OF THE HEART

ROBERT PETER JACOBY, M.S., LPC-S
BRIAN MACGREGOR, BFA

THE MASTER KEY PRESS ASHEVILLE NORTH CAROLINA

1

THE MASTER KEY PRESS
BLACK MOUNTAIN, NORTH CAROLINA

ISBN Paperback   **978-0-615-36995-2**

ISBN Hardback   **978-0-9915068-9-7**

ISBN E-book   **978-0-615-82307-2**

Published by   : The Master Key Press ; www.masterkeypress.com

E-mail   : themaptolove@yahoo.com

Website   : www.TheMapToLOVE.com

Contact the above address to order, or call/fax/e-mail for more information about this book.

Credits

Concept:	Robert Jacoby
Artwork:	Brian MacGregor
Edited by:	Jan Thomas, Mark Garner, Katie Hornowski, Jennifer Flynn, Tom Dennard, Kathy Ponte
Typesetting/design/layout by:	R. Jacoby, B. MacGregor, J. Flynn, Kimberly Lewis

ARTWORK AS IT APPEARS:

ALL ARTWORK, PRINTS, AND COMMISSIONS AVAILABLE AT
WWW. BRIAN-MACGREGOR.COM

TO THE ETERNAL

ONE;

THANK YOU FOR LOVE.

TO MY BELOVED DAUGHTER
ISADORA;
THANK YOU FOR LOVING ME , AND TEACHING ME HOW TO LOVE EVEN MORE
THAN I COULD HAVE EVER IMAGINED.

TO DANIELLE FOR YOUR LOVE, PATIENCE, HUMOR AND COMPASSION

TO MY FAMILY- BY BIRTH AND BY HEART-
I LOVE YOU.
I TREASURE ALL THAT YOU HAVE TAUGHT ME,
AND STILL TEACH ME TO THIS DAY.

TO ALL OF MY DEAR FRIENDS;
THANK YOU FOR ALL OF YOUR LAUGHTER,
LOVE, AND MOST OF ALL YOUR SUPPORT OVER THE YEARS.
I TREASURE EVERY MOMENT WE'VE SPENT TOGETHER.

And most of all....

HONOR TO YOU
GREAT WARRIORS OF LOVE,
MIGHTY SOLDIERS OF PEACE,

PAST,
PRESENT,
FUTURE.

THANK YOU.

IN YOUR
NAME,
WE LIVE TO
LOVE
ANOTHER DAY.

Chapters

A Gentle (but serious) Word of Caution

What you are about to read will change your perspective on Life, Love, and the Art of Living in the Present Moment. Yes—living in the present is in fact an art form. This manual has brought an abundance of Health, Happiness, and Wealth to countless people. You are the next person.

It is important to know that there is a simple, yet profound, formula to change ones Reality (The *Now*). By changing the way that you think, you change the way that you live. This manual will change your thoughts, thereby changing the way you view and interact with the world around you. In fact, if the world were a series of locked doors, you now have the Master Key.

Your Reality is based on your actions. Your actions are fueled by your emotions. Your emotions are created by your thoughts—and more often than not—your thoughts are based on your core beliefs. These core beliefs are programmed into your subconscious—by your parents, society, media, religious/spiritual beliefs, culture, etc. In fact, you are probably unaware of many of your core beliefs. Most of us are. Amazing (and partially terrifying) to think that the life we are living may not be what we are creating, but what we are *RE*-creating based on who we've been conditioned to become. The good news is that you can change that…now.

The Map to Love is many things—a survival guide, a map, a compass, a text book on human psychology, a primer on the art of psychotherapy, counseling, and, of course, parenting—as well as a tool to inspire you on the days when your negative thoughts are outweighing the positive ones. It's what you need it to be, at the precise moment that you need it.

Depending on where you are in your journey and how much you need to change your destructive thoughts, your heart will let you know how much and how often you need to re-read The Map to Love. Is your heart aching? Read it three times a day for 30 days (twice in silence, and the third time aloud.) Do you need a reframe in your life? Read this every morning or at the end of your day. Need a quick pick me up? Ask a question, and then "randomly" turn to a page (or two, or three). Feel lost? Refer to the map at the center of this book. You will know what you need at the exact time that you need it.

Congratulations. You are about to see things very differently.

LOVE

Yep...

That's THE answer!

So what's the question....
well,

you know

the ones that

EVERYONE

eventually asks...

Who am I?

What is the purpose of life?

Where did I come from?

What am I really made of?

What am I looking for?

What makes me happy?

What am I running from?

Where do I go when I die?

Why am I reading this book?

_____
(add your ? here)

WHY ARE WE HERE??

the answer....

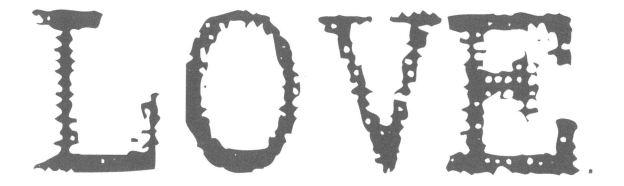

LOVE

It's the reason for all things.
EVERYTHING.

LOVE is the answer,
the question, *and* the mystery.

It is LOVE that brought you into this
world.
LOVE drives you, LOVE confuses you.
It is LOVE you hunger for.

You exist for LOVE...
...and when you die,
you return to LOVE.

LOVE is not just another emotion in the
game of life.

LOVE *IS THE GAME*.

Without LOVE, life would be a painful
journey toward nowhere.

LOVE

takes many forms.

Attraction, passion, and desire
are only a few of the creative
manifestations of LOVE.

Hate, prejudice, and jealousy
are only a few of the destructive
manifestations of LOVE.

Plain and simple...
we are either
CREATING LOVE or DESTROYING LOVE.

Reading this book means one thing....
You are ready to return to creating more LOVE in
your life and the lives around you!

Let's start from the beginning,

well, at least the beginning of you...

Once you arrived into this world
you were LOVED by your parents, or parent
(as best as he/she/they could have),
and spent your childhood playing,

Playing = HAVING FUN

FUN = LOVING THE MOMENT

FUN IS LOVE

You start your life
PLAYING WITH LOVE

When you are having FUN, there is no
thinking about the past or the future
There is just the

NOW...

Then you grow a little older

(not up),

and spend the rest of your life

searching for,

running from,

or better yet..

LIVING IN...

(You guessed it)

LOVE.

When we are

IN LOVE,

with ourselves,
with another,
with everything...

Time Stops

It ceases to exist

We transcend time

We become ONE with the moment

It's like when we are engaged in a

deep passionate kiss,

and then we stop; next thing we know...

Sooo much Time has passed.

We get lost in the Moment, or
maybe it's

THE

ॐ

Om-ment

Either way...

We get passionately,
deliciously,
and infinitely

LOST IN LOVE.

Conversely, when we are not LIVING IN LOVE

(I.E. DEPRESSION, ANXIETY, CONFLICT, TURMOIL, FEAR, ANGER,
JEALOUSY, HATRED, GREED, ETC...)

We Feel Lost.

WE MISTAKENLY BELIEVE THAT WE ARE EITHER

LOST IN LOVE
OR
IN SEARCH OF LOVE

THE TRUTH IS,
YOU ARE NEVER REALLY LOST FROM LOVE
BECAUSE…

THE OPPORTUNITY TO FEEL LOVE IN EVERY MOMENT IS INHERENT

IN ALL OF US.

THE REASON WE ARE HERE

IS

TO PLAY WITH LOVE

BECAUSE

IT'S ALL LOVE

AND

LOVE IS ALL THERE IS.

THAT IS …

TO EXPERIENCE LOVE

AS OFTEN AS WE CAN,

AS INTENSELY AS WE CAN,

FOR

AS LONG AS WE CAN.

IN OTHER WORDS...

WE ARE HERE TO APPRECIATE THE INTENSE EXPERIENCE OF

LOVE

AT

EVERY SECOND.

in a nut shell...

WE LIVE FOR LOVE

WHAT ELSE IS THERE TO LIVE FOR?

IF YOU ARE NOT LOVING YOUR LIFE,
THEN
YOU ARE WASTING YOUR TIME.

REMEMBER,

YOUR TIME HERE IS LIMITED,
AND
IS SLIPPING AWAY WITH

each passing moment.

THE REAL QUESTION IS...

ARE YOU LIVING IN LOVE?

If you thought about that

then

YOU JUST MISSED IT!

(Poof!!!)

Ok, so let's find it....

The following manual contains

THE MAP TO LOVE.

The instructions on how to
Navigate The Art Of The HeART
in order to continue, return to, or begin

Living,
and
LOVING...

YOURSELF,
&
EVERYONE,
&
EVERYTHING.

(NOW)

And...

Since
LOVE
is
EVERYTHING

&

THE MASTER KEY

to

Attracting all things,

Then you are about to become...

WAIT FOR IT....................,

A LOVE Magnet!

So where do we start?...

HOW ABOUT NOW,

Yep...

CHAPTER I

THE EMOTIONAL COMPASS

Reality is brought to you in part by the TIME - SPACE CONTINUUM®. Time is a measurement, and constantly moving. As time unfolds, everything in space changes. *Reality* is always changing. *Reality* is in a constant state of change within the theater of TIME & SPACE. Nothing stands still.

Everything is always moving, growing, and transforming.

EVERYTHING, INCLUDING YOU!

Without delving into the science and mechanics of the mysterious TIME - SPACE CONTINUUM®, there are only a few things you *need* to know. We perceive TIME in three places: PAST, PRESENT, and FUTURE. Our minds surf TIME much like a pendulum. We know this because that is how our consciousness swings through *Reality* - from the PAST, to the PRESENT, to the FUTURE, PRESENT, PAST, and over again. Back and forth, all day long. However, you actually exist in only one place..

NOW

You'll also notice that if you let it swing out of control on its own, it will spend more time in the PAST and FUTURE, than in the PRESENT. The PAST is our *History*, the FUTURE our *Fantasy*, and the PRESENT moment, **NOW**, is *Reality*.

Reality is
NOW.
History and *Fantasy*
are not *Reality*.
Poof!
You just missed it.
Thinking about it
means you tried to
grab it. When we try
to hold on to time, or
things in time, we end
up missing
NOW.

TO LIVE IN LOVE IS TO STAY IN THE PRESENT.

Holding on is doing, and doing is not being.

The only way to prepare for the FUTURE is by being in the

NOW,

THE closest place to the FUTURE you can get.

If we worry about the FUTURE,

based on our experience of the PAST,

we are missing where we are...

WHICH IS

NOW

As many in *Reality* have already said, the moment right

NOW

is a gift from the universe, and that's why it's

THE PRESENT.

THIS VERY MOMENT IS THE ONLY PLACE IN

THE GAME OF LOVE

THAT YOU, THE PLAYER, HAS *ANY*

CONTROL...

CONTROL

OF YOUR ACTIONS IN,

AND

AWARENESS

OF,

THE EVER PRESENT MOMENT.

THE EMOTIONAL COMPASS

There is only one real feeling of being....LOVE

EVERY FEELING, OR "EMOTION", OTHER THAN LOVE IS ACTUALLY THE HEART SIGNALING TO US THAT WE HAVE MOVED AWAY FROM THE MOMENT, AWAY FROM BEING LOVE.

THE TRUE NORTH OF THE HEART.

THERE IS ONLY ONE REAL FEELING....

LOVE

EVERY OTHER "FEELING" IS ACTUALLY AN EMOTION
WHICH IS A DEGREE, OR PIECE OF...

LOVE.

OUR E-MOTIONS ARE ACTUALLY PARTS OF OUR
INTERNAL COMPASS WHICH ARE
E-MOTIONING, OR EVER-MOTIONING US BACK TO

LOVE

OUR E-MOTIONS TELL US WHERE WE ARE, AND WHERE WE WANT
TO BE.
TIME AND E-MOTIONS ARE THE TWO THINGS THAT WE CANNOT
ESCAPE WHILE WE ARE ALIVE.
IN ESSENCE, OUR LIVES ARE MOMENTS OF

LOVE,

LIFE = MOMENTS OF LOVE
(a.k.a. FUN)

TIME AND E-MOTIONS

ARE ALWAYS WORKING TOGETHER TO

HELP YOU RETURN TO THE PRESENT;

WHERE WE COMPLETELY EXPERIENCE

THE FEELING

LOVE

BECAUSE.....

EMOTIONS ARE ACTUALLY PLACES IN TIME

IF YOU SPEND TOO MUCH TIME IN THE PAST, SADNESS, GRIEF, SHAME, AND GUILT WILL BECOME YOUR *REALITY*. ALL OF WHICH ARE EMOTIONS THAT *SLOW DOWN* TIME.

STAYING IN THE PAST
SLOWS DOWN TIME

THAT'S WHY WHEN YOU DWELL ON THE PAIN THAT YOU HAVE EXPERIENCED IN YOUR LIFE YOU FEEL...

HEAVY, SAD, DEPRESSED, WEIGHTED, DOWN, SHAMEFUL, GUILTY, REGRETFUL, BLAH

THE EVENTS THAT CAUSED THESE EMOTIONS HAVE PASSED. THEY ARE IN THE PAST. YOU CANNOT DO ANYTHING MORE WITH THEM EXCEPT HEAL, LET GO, AND MOVE ON.
RETURN TO NOW

(Remember....EVERYTHING HAPPENS FOR A REASON.)

IF YOU SPEND TOO MUCH TIME IN THE FUTURE, FEAR, WORRY, AND ANXIETY BECOME YOUR *REALITY.* ALL OF WHICH ARE EMOTIONS THAT *SPEED UP* TIME.

STAYING IN THE FUTURE
SPEEDS UP TIME

THAT'S WHY WHEN YOU CONSTANTLY LIVE IN AND WORRY ABOUT THE FUTURE, YOU FEEL....

ANXIOUS, FEARFUL, STRESSED, WORRIED
PANICKED, TERRIFIED,

ARGH

THE IMAGINED EVENTS THAT CAN CAUSE THESE EMOTIONS HAVE NOT HAPPENED, AND MAY NEVER HAPPEN. ALTHOUGH YOU CREATED THE IMAGINED FEARS IN THE FUTURE *(BASED ON WHAT HAPPENED TO YOU OR SOMEONE ELSE IN THE PAST),* YOU CANNOT DO ANYTHING MORE WITH THEM THAN TO STAY IN THE PRESENT AND LET THEM GO.

(Remember....YOU ARE CREATING YOUR REALITY.)

TO AVOID THESE NEGATIVE EMOTIONS,
OR AT LEAST TO KEEP THEM TO A MINIMUM,
BREATHE, FOCUS & KEEP
THE PENDULUM IN YOUR MIND STILL.
BE

-NOW-

in the present

THE ONLY PLACE THAT *REALITY* IS HAPPENING.

THE TRUE HOME OF LOVE

&❧ EMOTIONS ARE THE COMPASS OF THE SOUL ❧&

CHAPTER II

THE BEAUTY OF PAIN

Both PAIN and LOVE are our primary
teachers. The only difference is that PAIN
teaches at a *painful speed.*

is

THE

road sign in our lives, telling us we have moved
away from the moment, and from

LOVE

PAIN also tells us the degree to which we have
LOVED
someone or something after it is gone.

THERE ARE

2

SOURCES OF HEARTACHE

1.PAIN

2.SUFFERING

1. <u>PAIN</u> IS A PART OF LIFE!

THINGS BREAK,
STUFF FALLS APART
PEOPLE ABUSE US INTENTIONALLY
PEOPLE HURT US UNINTENTIONALLY
LIVING THINGS DIE

THERE ARE 5 FORMS OF THIS PAIN
they are:

1. PHYSICAL PAIN
2. EMOTIONAL/PSYCHOLOGICAL/SPIRITUAL PAIN
3. SEXUAL/GENDER ROLE PAIN
4. NEGLECT/BROKEN HEART/LONELINESS PAIN
5. BOREDOM

When we experience the Pain that is inherent in life, all we can do is grieve, heal, and LOVE some more. This pain will not last forever (that is if you let it go).

REMEMBER...

TIME HEALS

AND

REVEALS

ALL

THINGS

AND

PAIN IS ACTUALLY TEACHING US HOW TO LOVE

SOME MORE

YEP....

THE MORE YOU LOVE SOMETHING
THE MORE PAIN YOU FEEL WHEN IT'S GONE.

PAIN

Is

Actually a Form

Of

LOVE

WHETHER YOU HAVE LOST YOURSELF, SOMETHING, OR SOMEONE ELSE -

PAIN IS THE MEASURE OF HOW MUCH YOU HAVE

TRULY

LOVED

2. <u>SUFFERING</u> IS WHAT WE CREATE!

The HEARTACHE that we create out of FEAR and DENIAL
of looking at the original source of our PAIN
(a.k.a. abuse) is called SUFFERING.

WE CREATE SUFFERING.

WE CREATE OUR OWN SUFFERING WHEN WE CHOOSE TO NOT DEAL WITH THE PAIN THAT LIFE THROWS AT US.

For example....

You get hurt by yourself or someone else by being
physically, sexually, emotionally abused or neglected,
tortured, broken hearted, disconnected, spiritually
lost, or just bored, or someone you LOVE dies, or
something breaks, or something really crazy happens, or
you experience trauma, or you survive war and combat,
and you decide that...

YOU JUST CANNOT DEAL WITH THIS PAIN....

In that exact moment

YOU

then begin to

CREATE

more PAIN through

SUFFERING,

in order to create a much more painful
distraction, to keep yourself from
facing the original experience of
PAIN & ABUSE.

How?....well..You create suffering through...

ABUSING DRUGS AND ALCOHOL
ENGAGING IN DESTRUCTIVE RELATIONSHIPS
SEEKING DISTRACTIONS LIKE
TV, OVEREATING, GAMBLING,
SEX (WITHOUT LOVE),

DRAMA

(DESTRUCTIVE REACTIONS AND MANIPULATIVE ACTIONS),
CHAOS, GOSSIP,
SELF DESTRUCTIVE BEHAVIORS,
AVOIDING OTHERS
AVOIDING LIFE ALTOGETHER,
AND ON, AND ON, AND ON...

_____

(ADD YOUR OWN HERE)

GREAT, NOW WHAT...............

Simple...

YOU RETURN TO LOVE

❧ PAIN IS TEACHING YOU TO LOVE SOME MORE ❧

CHAPTER III

THE LADDER OF LOVE

THE LADDER OF LOVE

YOU ARE BORN WITH THE
KNOWLEDGE OF HOW TO
LIVE IN, AND RETURN TO,

LOVE,

&

YOU HAVE BEEN
TRANSFORMING PAIN
INTO
LOVE
FROM THE DAY YOU WERE
BORN.

IN TIMES OF COMPLEX PAIN, AND GREAT FEAR, IT IS EASY TO LOSE
SIGHT OF THE WAY BACK TO
LOVE.

Returning to LOVE is like riding a bicycle.
Once you have learned how,
It becomes second nature each time you
get back on.....

NO MATTER HOW LONG IT'S BEEN SINCE YOU'VE RIDDEN A BIKE

LET'S SEE HOW THIS WORKS:

Day 1: Imagine that you were just born, and you are now exploring your world. You are curious, so you begin to touch everything. As you go near the stove, your mother yells "DON'T TOUCH THAT!" Do you listen? Probably not. Why? Because we often like to experience things for ourselves.

OUR BELIEFS ARE FORMED IN THREE WAYS:

- Teachings   (Minimal Consequences)

- Observation   (Moderate Consequences)

- Personal Experience (Severe   Consequences)

Which of these is the most poignant?...

If you are one of the curious (or *Stubborn*) ones, then

PERSONAL

EXPERIENCE

of course.

Now, let's say the stove was NOT on - it wasn't hot when you touched it. What have you learned? Nothing. Except the erroneous belief that your Mother doesn't know what she is talking about.

Day 2: You have a whole day's worth of experience under your belt, and of course believe that you know everything there is to know about *Reality*. You walk up to the stove and challenge the monster that your mother oh so fears.

"I TOLD YOU NOT TO TOUCH THAT!!!" she screams from the wings. Courageously, you throw your cape over your shoulder, and engage the steel beast. You touch it, and again it is not on. What have you learned?

That your mother is twice as CRAZY as she was yesterday...

Day 3: And you're off. Screaming about the house, touching everything in sight, occasionally putting corner lint and small toy pieces in your mouth. No problem. Until you get to the stove. The drill is the same.

YOU WALK UP. MOM YELLS, "DON'T TOUCH THAT!"

YOU TOUCH IT,

(ignoring the panic of your twice mistaken mentor.)

TODAY THE STOVE IS ON, AND IT'S HOT.

YOU GET BURNED.

GETTING BURNED = PAIN.

NOW YOU REALIZE THAT YOU HAVE MADE A BIG MISTAKE.

(NOTE: IN CASES OF ABUSE, THE MISTAKE IS MADE BY THE ABUSER!)

MISTAKES ARE WHAT WE CALL THE COMPLETE EXPERIENCE OF

PAIN.

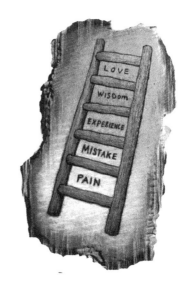

THE LESSON IS NOT OVER, REMEMBER,
SO FAR YOU HAVE ONLY TRAVELED UP
THE FIRST TWO PARTS OF THE LADDER;
PAIN → MISTAKE.

Day 4: Today is different. In fact, *very different*. A great lesson is about to unfold. As you come near the stove you take a quick turn towards the toy chest, and avoid the stove altogether. Does your mom need to say anything? Not at all. THE LADDER OF LOVE has done its job. As you walked near the stove you remembered the **EXPERIENCE** from yesterday, it made you **WISE** to the dangers of the stove. Today you experience **HAPPINESS**, a degree of **LOVE**, because you did not get burned.

You have successfully learned to
climb up the ladder
(again).

YOU ARE

HAPPY

(A DEGREE OF LOVE)

BECAUSE YOU HAD THE

WISDOM

TO AVOID GETTING BURNED AGAIN BY THE STOVE.

THAT

WISDOM

WAS BASED ON YOUR

EXPERIENCE

WITH THE STOVE, BUT NOT JUST ANY EXPERIENCE. IT WAS THE

MISTAKE

YOU MADE BECAUSE YOU WERE BURNED.

THAT BURN CAUSED YOU

PAIN.

THANK YOU PAIN

FOR TEACHING ME NOT TO GO NEAR THE STOVE.

Remember, you will see that stove again in your life, only next time it may look different. Next time it may be a person, place, thing, event, experience, etc....

Each time we allow ourselves to face and heal our pain, instead of creating more suffering to avoid looking at that pain, we LEARN how to avoid the same situation in the future.

Isn't it amazing how the ladder works?

Even more amazing is you have been using this ladder all of your life!

Sometimes you climb it quickly, sometimes slowly.

Either way; you have always been climbing it.

Could you have avoided the whole thing? Yes, by using the other two learning styles - teaching and/or observation. Your mother *taught* you not to touch the stove. You just didn't listen. Had you stood near the stove long enough you might have *observed* someone else get burned.

But no, you had to *experience* it for yourself.

Good for you!

As painful as the stove was,
IT HAS BEEN A POWERFUL TEACHER!

THE POINT...

THINGS THAT HURT THE MOST ARE OUR MOST POWERFUL TEACHERS.

Now if anyone asks about the stove, you know what you are talking about.

Besides, we are here to experience *Reality*, not just hear about it, or watch it pass by.

Now you know what to do next time you see the stove –

Because YOU have LEARNED from it.

IN FACT...

YOU MAY SOMEDAY BE ABLE TO HELP SOMEONE ELSE NOT GET BURNED

So what do you do with the
PAIN,
now that you have moved up the ladder to
LOVE?

LET IT GO!

THIS IS A CRUCIAL MOVE IN THE GAME.

LET PAIN GO.

IF YOU ARE HOLDING ONTO PAIN, YOU ARE ACTUALLY LIVING IN THE PAST.

LOVE IS EXPERIENCED IN THE PRESENT,

(REMEMBER.)

Living in the past causes more PAIN...

AFTER YOU HEAL THE

PAIN

AND ACKNOWLDEGE THE

MISTAKE

ONLY THEN CAN YOU ADD THE

EXPERIENCE

TO YOUR MEMORY BANK OF LIFE'S

WISDOM.

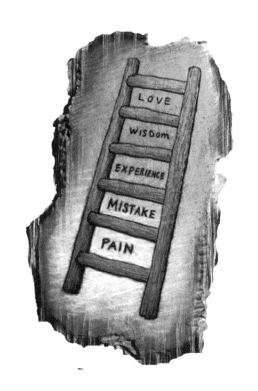

IF LATER IN LIFE YOU ARE FACED WITH A SIMILAR CHALLENGE, YOU NOW HAVE THE TOOLS TO MEET THAT CHALLENGE SUCCESSFULLY AND ADVANCE TO

LOVE.

THE MAIN REASON PEOPLE DO NOT LET GO OF **PAIN** IS BECAUSE **PAIN** SOMETIMES LEAVES BEHIND **SHAME, GUILT, REGRET, PANIC, WORRY,** AND **FEAR.** THESE EMOTIONS ARE REALLY **PAIN** IN DISGUISE. IF YOU HOLD ON TO THEM, YOU ARE REALLY HOLDING ONTO **PAIN** –

PAIN PREVENTS YOU FROM MOVING UP THE LADDER OF LOVE.

When we release ourselves from the
Shackles
of
PAIN

We open our hearts to the presence of

❧ LOVE IS THE ANTIDOTE FOR PAIN ❧

CHAPTER IV

THE BROKEN HEART

SO, you

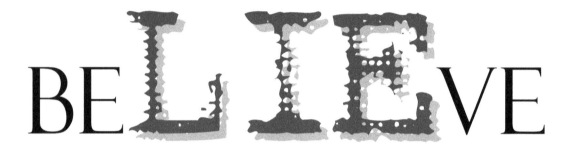

BELIEVE

THAT YOU HAVE
A
BROKEN HEART,

WELL………

YOUR

HEART

IS

NOT

BROKEN

Nope!

Your
EMOTIONAL HEART,
The center of your soul,
The place from which you

GIVE & RECEIVE LOVE...

CANNOT

BE

BROKEN...

NEVER!

Ever...

When you feel that your heart is

Breaking

Or

Broken

Or even

Torn,

Shattered

&

Destroyed...

...It is your LOVE that you are feeling

&

YOUR

LOVE

IS

INDESTRUCTABLE

What YOU ARE actually

FEELING,

Is not a breaking, but

A

BUILDING

A

STRETCHING

GROWING

BUILDING

Of...

yep

You guessed it...

LOVE...

Is A Changing
STRETCHING-GROWING-BUILDING
HEART PAINFUL?

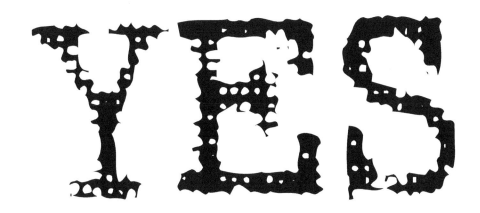

YES

BUT…………..

This is how

your

HEART

BECOMES

STRONG

Your

LOVE

Is

like every other muscle in your

PHYSICAL

EMOTIONAL

AND

SPIRITUAL

BODY

Muscle Becomes

STRONG

ONLY when it is first

RIPPED,

STRETCHED,
&
TORN APART

IRONICALLY,

It is the Loss of

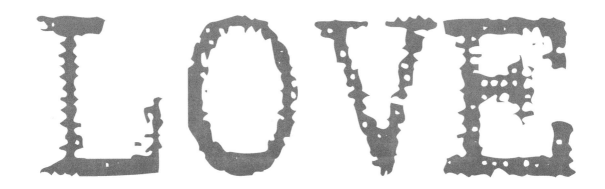

LOVE

WHICH

STRENGTHENS

YOUR

HEART

YES, IRONICALLY…

DEATH

DIVORCE

SEPARATION

UNKNOWING

ANTICIPATION

ABANDONEMENT

BETRAYAL

PAIN

SUFFERING

ABUSE

HUNGER

COMBAT

WAR

TORTURE

AND ON AND ON ...

These are in fact the

BUILDING BLOCKS,

THE

FOUNDATIONS,

The
Seeds TO THE

DEPTHS

OF YOUR

LOVE.

These are the ways in which your heart
STRETCHES,
OPENS,
AND FLOURISHES

So that YOU can...

...ULTIMATELY

LOVE

EVEN

MORE

Without the experience of SOUR,
there is no SWEET;
Without the experience of BITTER,
there is no BLAND;
Without the experience of SILENCE,
there is no MUSIC;
Without the true experience of
PAIN, there is no true
HUMBLE, GENTLE, and FRAGILE
appreciation
of

LOVE

❧ PAIN IS WHAT MAKES LOVE GROW STRONG ❦

CHAPTER V

THE GAME OF LOVE

Just as any game on the toy store shelf,

THE GAME OF LOVE

has *only* four playing options:

1.   PLAY   LOVE

2.   Cheat   LOVE

3.   Deceive   LOVE

4.   Quit   LOVE

THE DIFFERENCE BETWEEN THESE OPTIONS IS BASED

SOLELY ON YOUR DECISION TO

CREATE LOVE OR DESTROY LOVE

AT EACH MOMENT OF YOUR *REALITY.*

1. PLAY LOVE

THIS OPTION IS THE CHOICE OF ALL

LOVERS,

Mystics, Masters, Sages, Seekers,
Warriors, Wanderers, Peacemakers,
Pupils, Healers, Teachers, Ragpickers...
and now
YOU,

BECAUSE IT IS THE ONLY OPTION THAT ALLOWS FOR THE
CREATION OF LOVE.
IT IS ALSO KNOWN AS

Being In Love.

1. PLAY LOVE

CHOOSING THIS OPTION, YOU AGREE TO JOYOUSLY PARTICIPATE
IN THE GAME OF LOVE, AND PLAY/LOVE/LIVE IN THIS MOMENT;
THE NOW!
LIVING LIFE ON LIFE'S TERMS, YOU ACCEPT EVENTS AS THEY
UNFOLD, AND REACT ACCORDINGLY (INTUITIVELY).
THIS OPTION IS CHARACTERIZED BY ALLOWING YOURSELF TO

BE AT

ONE

AND AWARE OF
THE EVER PRESENT MOMENT THROUGHOUT THE EXPERIENCE OF
THE GAME OF LOVE,
PLAYING THE GAME OF LOVE IS ALSO CHARACTERIZED BY QUICKLY
TRANSFORMING PAIN INTO LOVE.

❧THERE IS FAITH, COURAGE, PASSION, PATIENCE, AND
LOVE IN THE HEART OF THIS PLAYER ❧

🕷 NOTE 🕷

ATTEMPTING TO GAIN CONTROL OVER

THE GAME OF LOVE

AS WELL AS OTHER PLAYERS IN THE GAME,

IS A REACTION TO ABUSE, NEGLECT, AND GENERAL

LOSS OF TRUST IN LOVE DURING YOUR PART IN

THE GAME OF LOVE,

IT IS ALSO A SIGN THAT YOU ARE DESTROYING LOVE

AND ARE

NOW

CREATING SUFFERING.

TO ACTIVELY PLAY

THE GAME OF LOVE,

OR TO

BE IN LOVE,

MEANS YOU ARE WILLING TO MEET THE CHALLENGES

&

LEARN FROM THE LESSONS THAT YOU

&

THE GAME OF LOVE,

ARE CREATING

(together).

THE ONLY CONTROL YOU USE IS TO KEEP YOUR

AWARENESS IN THE PRESENT MOMENT

&

CREATE MORE LOVE.

THE FOLLOWING OPTIONS

ARE THE WAYS IN WHICH WE

WILL

NO LONGER

PLAY

THE GAME OF LOVE

NO LONGER WILL WE EVER...

2. CHEAT LOVE: Those who **Cheat** LOVE are

characterized by having a lack of patience and tolerance for challenges and pain. Cheaters take power, money, and resources from other players in order to move their own agenda forward and escape from themselves as well as *Reality*. They have given up the belief that life, LOVE, will provide them with what they need (*not want*!), and tend to feel they deserve more than the gifts they have been presented with, because they do not see the complexity and LOVE in each PRESENT MOMENT.

CHEATERS

Are playing THE GAME OF LOVE at the expense of others.

THERE IS NO FAITH IN THE HEART OF THIS PLAYER.

3.DECEIVE LOVE:

Those who **Deceive** LOVE are characterized by creating their own game, nightmare or fantasy, within the true and only game of *Reality:* THE GAME OF LOVE. Deceivers, or Pretenders, or Manipulators, are playing two or more games or agendas at the same time. Deceivers <u>appear</u> to be actively involved in creating LOVE and participating in *Reality.* However, behind their complex system of walls, disguises, and manipulations, they are playing according to an entirely different set of rules; their own. Whether they are consciously aware of it or not.

DECEIVERS

Are playing their own game within
THE GAME OF LOVE.

THERE IS NO HONOR IN THE HEART OF THIS PLAYER

4.QUIT LOVE:

This option is exactly what it sounds like: A complete quitting, and withdrawal from playing THE GAME OF LOVE. Quitters make minimal effort to engage *Reality,* if at all. Quitters withdraw from *Reality,* become reclusive, and try to remain within the comfort of their surroundings. Simply put, Quitters do not care to play anymore. The idea of active participation in THE GAME OF LOVE is replaced with common addictions, and other forms of escape. Addictions are nothing more than doing the same thing repeatedly, for long periods of time, thus ignoring the game and the players in it (a.k.a. LOVE).

QUITTERS

Are waiting for THE GAME OF LOVE to end.

THERE IS NO HOPE NOR PASSION IN THE HEART OF THIS PLAYER.

A NOTE ON OPTIONS 2, 3, & 4.

```
2.   Cheat    LOVE
3.   Deceive  LOVE
4.   Quit     LOVE
```

THERE ARE MANY PLAYERS, WHO HAVE CREATED,

AND ARE NOW LIVING IN, THEIR OWN WORLDS;

a

FANTASY or NIGHTMARE

within

THE GAME OF LOVE,

THIS PHENOMENON HAPPENS WHEN ABUSED HUMANS

(WHICH AT SOME POINT IS ALL OF US)

HAVE NOT HEALED AND RECOVERED FROM THEIR ABUSE, TRAUMAS,

AND/OR LOSS. THIS IN TURN RESULTS IN FEARING FUTURE LOSS OF

CONTROL OF THE GAME (A.K.A LOVE), THEREFORE CREATING A NEW,

TWISTED, AND PAINFUL REALITY.

THE PLAYER WHO CHOOSES TO...

2.   Cheat   LOVE
3.   Deceive   LOVE
4.   Quit   LOVE

HAS EXPERIENCED PAIN AND NOW

WILLFULLY REFUSES

TO FACE THE LOSS, HEAL,

AND BE VULNERABLE ONCE AGAIN.

THOSE WHO

Cheat LOVE, Deceive LOVE, or Quit LOVE,

USE A GREAT DEAL OF DESTRUCTIVE ENERGY

IN AN ILLUSORY ATTEMPT TO CONTROL AND DESTROY

LOVE.

(AS WELL AS CONTROL OTHERS IN *REALITY.*)

FOR EXAMPLE: IF YOU HAVE BEEN HURT IN *REALITY*,

AND YOU CHOOSE TO NOT LET GO OF PAIN,

THEN YOU WILL TRY TO CONTROL

THE GAME OF LOVE

BY OPTING TO

Cheat LOVE,

(A form of Suffering)

Deceive LOVE,

(A form of Suffering)

Quit LOVE

(A form of Suffering)

OR ANY COMBINATION OF THE THREE.

YOU WILL EXPERIENCE PAIN.

HOWEVER,

RESISTING THE GRIEF PROCESS,

HEALING, AND FEELING YOUR HEART EXPANDING

(HEARTACHE), DURING CHALLENGING MOMENTS THROUGHOUT

THE GAME OF LOVE,

WILL ONLY LEAD YOU TO CHOOSE TO

Cheat LOVE, Deceive LOVE, or Quit LOVE.

IT IS, AGAIN, IRONIC THAT IF YOU RESIST PLAYING

THE GAME OF LOVE

(I.E. Cheat LOVE, Deceive LOVE, Quit LOVE),

THE GAME OF LOVE ONLY BECOMES MORE CHALLENGING TO PLAY,

FORCING YOU AT SOME POINT TO LET GO OF CONTROL,

SURRENDER, AND OPEN YOUR HEART TO ITS TRUE NATURE –

LOVE.

❧ LOVE IS THE GAME ❧

CHAPTER VI

FOLLOWING INTUITION

INTUITION

IS

KNOWING THAT YOU KNOW.

Knowing what you ask?

Well,

KNOWING

THAT YOU
KNOW
EVERYTHING

Yes, everything!

YOU,

Just as ALL of the creatures in this
AMAZING REALITY,
are born with the gift of
KNOWING...

Knowing how to look, hear, breathe, walk,
communicate, eat, create, dream, think, analyze,
compute, problem solve, make nests, make webs,
find food, find water, as well as make friends,
avoid danger,
and most importantly

LIVE IN LOVE.

But Wait, There's more!

There is much that INTUITION gives us,
but one of its most precious gifts is that
it tells us exactly what we need to know...

AT
THE PRECISE MOMENT
THAT WE NEED TO KNOW IT

...when to make a left, instead of a right...

...when to befriend someone we just met,
&
when to run from someone we have always known.

...when to start giving our heart to another,
&
WHEN TO TAKE IT BACK...

...when it is time to surrender to another, and trust,
or when it is time to create a boundary, or a fortress,

AND RAISE YOUR SHIELD!

INTUITION

tells us when to hold on, but also instructs us when it
is time to

LET GO

Intuition, or knowing, or "enlightenment" is listening
to, *and following,* the gentle rhythm of our life, the
path we should follow, the way, THE FORCE, the Tao;
the road less travelled.

It is the innate and most prized of our senses in that
it is ALWAYS pointing us back to Reducing
(not escaping)

PAIN

and

LIVING IN LOVE

Sometimes, and only sometimes, our FEAR of
facing our PAIN, takes us into
THE LABYRINTH OF SUFFERING.

Our FEAR of Loneliness, Lack, and yes..even
OF LOVE!

This LABYRINTH OF SUFFERING is filled with
Hatred, Drama, Chaos, Jealousy, Despair,
Hopelessness, fear, and anger...

Could your INTUITION lead you to
more suffering?

NO

It is your
Free Will, and Choices, based on FEAR that do,
HOWEVER...

It is your

INTUITION

That will ALWAYS lead you out of the
PATH OF DANGER & CHAOS.

It is your

INTUITION

That will ALWAYS guide you through
DARK & DESOLATE PLACES
&
It is your

INTUITION

THAT WILL ALWAYS CARRY YOU GENTLY OUT OF
THE LABYRINTH OF SUFFERING...
AND INTO THE ARMS OF

LOVE

❧ INTUITION TAKES US TO WHERE WE NEED TO BE ❧

CHAPTER VII

THE MAP TO LOVE

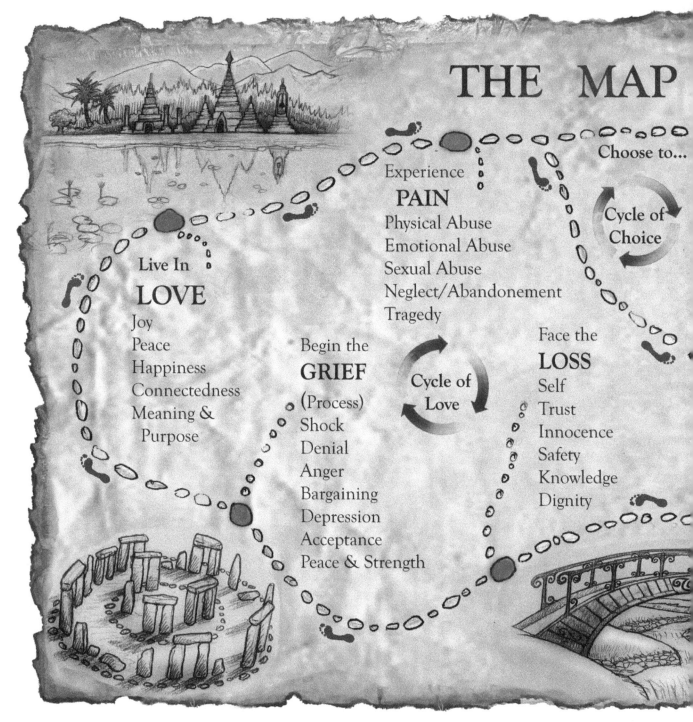

THE MAP

Choose to...

Experience
PAIN
Physical Abuse
Emotional Abuse
Sexual Abuse
Neglect/Abandonement
Tragedy

Cycle of
Choice

Live In
LOVE
Joy
Peace
Happiness
Connectedness
Meaning &
Purpose

Begin the
GRIEF
(Process)
Shock
Denial
Anger
Bargaining
Depression
Acceptance
Peace & Strength

Cycle of
Love

Face the
LOSS
Self
Trust
Innocence
Safety
Knowledge
Dignity

TO LOVE

Deny the
PAIN
Choose to Avoid
Looking at Your Pain
And Create Suffering
as a Distraction

Create
SUFFERING
(Through)
*Addictions
   Drugs & Alcohol
   Eating Disorders
   Relationships
   High Risk Behavior
*Violence to Self
   Cutting
   Self-Harm
*Violence To Others
   Physical
   Emotional
   Sexual

**Cycle of
Suffering**

Face the
PAIN
Choose to Begin the
Healing Process by
Accepting the Loss, and
Engage In Strengthening
your HeART

**Drama & Chaos
Hatred & Jealousy**

**Cycle of
Choice**

ROCK BOTTOM

Art by: Brian MacGregor   Concept by: Robert Jacoby

THE MAP TO LOVE

Navigational Instructions

1. Locate where you are on THE MAP TO LOVE

2. **IF YOU ARE LIVING IN LOVE:** Be grateful! You are Here NOW!
    Help those who need help through other areas of
    THE MAP TO LOVE so that they too can Be Here Now.

3. **IF YOU ARE EXPERIENCING PAIN:** Ask for help, find support,
    be still, and know: THIS TOO SHALL PASS. Collect the
    courage to Face the Pain, and Face the Loss, and allow
    yourself to flow with the river of grief as your heart
    heals and you RETURN TO LOVE; NOW.

NOTE:

REGARDLESS OF WHERE YOU ARE ON THE MAP TO LOVE,

YOU ARE ALWAYS IN LOVE. HOWEVER, THE REAL QUESTION IS...

ARE YOU HERE, NOW?

4. **IF YOU ARE DENYING YOUR PAIN:** STOP! Breathe, and Face Your
    Pain. The worst has happened. It is Facing the Loss and
    the grief process that you must now begin. The pulling you
    feel is LOVE calling you to return.

SURRENDER, AND RETURN TO NOW!

5. IF YOU ARE SUFFERING IN THE LABYRINTH OF SUFFERING:

STOP CREATING SUFFERING & FORGIVE.

A. STOP CREATING SUFFERING through abusing drugs, self-destruction, cutting, self-hatred, eating disorders, high-risk behaviors, violence, thoughts of suicide, DRAMA, Chaos, Greed, Hatred, ETC....(see map)

B. FORGIVE THOSE THAT HURT YOU. Realize that you created your own suffering because you were not ready to let go and forgive those that hurt you.

(NOT FOR THEM, BUT FOR YOURSELF!!!!!!)

C. FORGIVE YOURSELF. Stop punishing yourself (a.k.a suffering) for what happened to you, and what you did.

YOU DID THE BEST YOU COULD

WITH WHAT YOU HAD, AT THE TIME THAT YOU HAD IT!!!

D. FACE THE PAIN & ABUSE. Accept that you experienced physical, sexual, emotional abuse, neglect, broken heart, and loss. Loss of others, loss of dreams, loss of parts of yourself.

E. CHOOSE TO HEAL AND RECOVER. Engage in the healing process. See a therapist, a professional, or someone who knows how to help you *lead yourself* out of darkness. Talk to your family, a friend, a partner, but most of all, talk to YOURSELF!

BECOME A WARRIOR AND NO LONGER A VICTIM!

F. RETURN TO LIVING IN LOVE!

The choice to

LOVE NOW

takes only one second.

YES, ONE SECOND!

However,

it is every second after that which you
must choose the same thing time and time
again:

That is...

TO LIVE IN LOVE...

now

❧ LOVE IS THE GREATEST OF ALL JOURNEYS ❧

CHAPTER VIII

THE SECRET TO FINDING LOVE

AND NOW...

THE
SECRET
TO
FINDING
LOVE

Here it is...

GET READY!!

THERE

IS

NO

SECRET

BECAUSE...

LOVE

IS

ALL THERE IS,

in fact...

IT IS ALL LOVE...

ALL OF IT..

If we stand quietly,
and LISTEN,
and DREAM,
and HOPE,
and LOVE,
and HELP others,
and BELIEVE,
and then
most of all...

BE PATIENT

THEN...

WE CAN HEAR

THE TRUTH

THAT WE HAVE

BEEN

RUNNING TO,

PLAYING IN,

AND

RUNNING FROM

OUR ENTIRE LIVES

THAT TRUTH BEING ...

WE ARE LOVE

but...

You
Already
Knew
That

didn't you.

...In fact...

WE ALL
KNOW THAT!

The only question left is:

WHAT BEAUTIFUL CREATION ARE YOU
NOW ABOUT TO MAKE OUT OF
LOVE?

∽ YOU ARE LOVE ∽

The Author

Therapist, artist, survival instructor, and author Rob Jacoby draws upon all four areas of his life and experience to offer us *The Map to Love: How to Navigate the Art of the Heart,* a life-giving perspective on understanding the complexities of the emotional landscape, and most of all how to find love and fulfillment. His twenty year career helping people from all walks of life, from working in maximum security prisons to managing programs in some of the top adolescent psychiatric hospitals in the country counseling those suffering from extreme emotional problems gives this book its lived-in authority. His passion for creation, particularly painting and music, drives the spontaneity and rhythm of its prose and presentation. In between parenting his daughter, Rob currently works in residential therapeutic settings, private practice, and conducts workshops and seminars on Love, The Art of Counseling, Effective Parenting, Relationships, Equine Therapy, and Meditation.

Rob loves what he does, and spends most of his time trying to understand love.

He still has more questions than answers.

The Artist

Brian MacGregor's "Romantic Surrealist" oil paintings are inspired by the Collective Unconscious. He does this by collaging thousands of people's handwritten dreams that he has been collecting for over a decade into his art. His images come straight from his meditations, dreams, and international travels to surreal dream-like destinations all over the world.

MacGregor is a nationally recognized Fine Artist who established a gallery of his work in the heart of downtown Savannah, GA in 2004. He began studying art in Virginia, a short while in Great Britain, and then graduated from the Savannah College of Art and Design with an Illustration degree.

MacGregor has won multiple awards including the International IASD First Place Dream Art Award, National Congressional Art Award, and Best Artist of Savannah 2007, to name a few. He has done over a dozen solo gallery shows and countless group shows around the country. MacGregor's been interviewed by international and national magazines from the US to Australia, local TV news to NPR and several students of art in between.

"We quest after happiness as if it were a thing, when simply being creative is the true endurance of happiness."

Brian MacGregor

The

is

Vocatus atque non vocatus deus aderit

CPSIA information can be obtained
at www.ICGtesting.com
Printed in the USA
JSHW012013280920
8203JS00002B/18